The Constitution of
The State of Maine:
A Quick Reference Guide

Bootblack Budget Books
Copyright 2018 ©
ISBN-13: 978-1986435819
ISBN-10: 1986435814

Contents:

Preamble – Page 22

Article I: Declaration of Rights – Page 23

Section 1. Natural rights

Section 2. Power inherent in people

Section 3. Religious freedom; sects equal; religious tests prohibited; religious teachers

Section 4. Freedom of speech and publication; libel; truth given in evidence; jury determines law and fact

Section 5. Unreasonable searches prohibited

Section 6. Rights of persons accused

Section 6-A. Discrimination against persons prohibited

Section 7. No person to answer to certain crimes but on indictment; exceptions; juries

Section 8. No double jeopardy

Section 9. Sanguinary laws, excessive bail, cruel or unusual punishments prohibited

Section 10. Bailable offenses; habeas corpus

Section 11. Attainder, ex post facto and contract-impairment laws prohibited

Section 12. Treason; testimony of 2 witnesses

Section 13. Suspension of laws

Section 14. Corporal punishment under military law

Section 15. Right of petition

Section 16. To keep and bear arms

Section 17. Standing armies

Section 18. Quartering of soldiers on citizens

Section 19. Right of redress for injuries

Section 20. Trial by jury

Section 21. Private property, when to be taken

Section 22. Taxes

Section 23. Title of nobility prohibited; tenure of offices

Section 24. Other rights not impaired

Article II: Electors – Page 29

Section 1. Qualifications of electors; written ballot; military servicemen; students

Section 2. Electors exempt from arrests on election days

Section 3. Exemption from military duty

Section 4. Time of state election; absentee voting

Section 5. Voting machines

Article III: Distribution of Powers – Page 31

Section 1. Powers distributed

Section 2. To be kept separate

Article IV: Part First - House of Representatives – Page 32

Section 1. Legislative department; style of acts

Section 2. Number of Representatives; biennial terms; division of the State into districts for House of Representatives

Section 3. Submission of reapportionment plan to Clerk of House; Legislature's action on commission's plan

Section 4. Qualifications; residency requirement

Section 5. Election of Representatives; lists of votes delivered forthwith; lists of votes examined by Governor; summons of persons who appear to be elected; lists shall be laid before the House

Section 6. Vacancies

Section 7. To choose own officers

Section 8. Power of impeachment

Article IV: Part Second – Senate – Page 36

Section 1. Number of Senators

Section 2. Submission of reapportionment plan to Secretary of Senate; Legislature's action on commission's plan; division of State into Senatorial Districts; division by Supreme Judicial Court.

Section 3. Election of Senators; lists of votes delivered forthwith

Section 4. Lists of votes examined by Governor; summons to persons who appear to be elected

Section 5. Determination of Senators elected; procedure for filling vacancies

Section 6. Qualifications

Section 7. To try impeachments; limitation of judgment of impeachment; party liable to be tried and punished in court

Section 8. To choose own officers

Article IV: Part Third - Legislative Power – Page 39

Section 1. To meet annually; power of Legislature to convene itself at other times; extent of legislative power

Section 1-A. Legislature to establish Apportionment Commission; number of quorum; compensation of commission members; commission's budget; division among political parties

Section 2. Bills to be signed by the Governor; proceedings, in case the Governor disapproves; allowing the Governor 10 days to act on legislation

Section 2-A. Line-item veto of dollar amounts appearing in appropriation or allocation sections of legislative documents

Section 3. Each House the judge of its elections; majority, a quorum

Section 4. May punish and expel members

Section 5. Shall keep a journal; yeas and nays

Section 6. May punish for contempt

Section 7. Compensation; traveling expenses

Section 8. Members exempt from arrest; freedom of debate

Section 9. Either House may originate bills; revenue bills

Section 10. Members not to be appointed to certain offices

Section 11. Persons disqualified to be members

Section 12. Adjournments

Section 13. Special legislation

Section 14. Corporations, formed under general laws

Section 15. Constitutional conventions

Section 16. Acts become effective in 90 days after recess; exception; emergency bill defined

Section 17. Proceedings for people's veto

1. Petition procedure; petition for people's veto
2. Effect of referendum
3. Referral to electors; proclamation by Governor

Section 18. Direct initiative of legislation

1. Petition procedure
2. Referral to electors unless enacted by the Legislature without change; number of signatures necessary on direct initiative petitions; dating signatures on petitions; competing measures
3. Timing of elections; proclamation by Governor

Section 19. Effective date of measures approved by people; veto power limited.

Section 20. Meaning of words "electors," "people," "recess of Legislature," "statewide election," "measure," "circulator," and "written petition"; written petitions for people's veto; written petitions for direct initiative

Section 21. City council of any city may establish direct initiative and people's veto

Section 22. Election officers and officials, how governed

Section 23. Municipalities reimbursed annually

Article V: Part First - Executive Power – Page 54

Section 1. Governor

Section 2. Term of office; reelection eligibility

Section 3. Election; votes to be returned to Secretary of State; Secretary of State to lay lists before the Senate and House of Representatives; provision in case of tie

Section 4. Qualifications

Section 5. Disqualifications

Section 6. Compensation

Section 7. Commander in chief

Section 8. To appoint officers

Section 9. To give information and recommend measures

Section 10. May require information of any officer

Section 11. Power to pardon and remit penalties, etc.; conditions

Section 12. Shall enforce the laws

Section 13. Convene the Legislature on extraordinary occasions, and adjourn it in case of disagreement; may change the place of meeting

Section 14. Vacancy, how supplied

Section 15. Temporary mental or physical disability of Governor

Article V: Part Second – Secretary – Page 61

Section 1. Election

Section 1-A. Succession to the office of Secretary of State

Section 2. Records of State; deputies.

Section 3. Attend the Governor, Senate, and House

Article V: Part Third -Treasurer – Page 62

Section 1. Election

Section 1-A. Succession to the office of Treasurer

Section 2. Bond

Section 3. Not to engage in trade

Section 4. No money drawn except upon appropriation or allocation

Section 5. Bonding regulations; prohibiting use of proceeds from sale of bonds to fund current expenditures

Article VI: Judicial Power – Page 64

Section 1. Courts

Section 2. Compensation

Section 3. To give opinion when required by Governor or either Branch of the Legislature

Section 4. Tenure of judicial officers; 6-month holdover period

Section 5. Limitation on holding other office

Section 6. Judges and registers of probate, election and tenure; vacancies

Article VII: Military – Page 66

Section 1. Officers, how appointed

Section 2. Qualifications and selection

Section 3. Adjutant General

Section 4. Standard of organization, armament and discipline

Section 5. Persons exempt from military duty

Article VIII: Part First – Education – Page 68

Section 1. Legislature shall require towns to support public schools; duty of Legislature

Section 2. Authority to pledge the credit of the State and to issue bonds for loans to Maine students in higher education and their parents

Article VIII: Part Second - Municipal Home Rule – Page 69

Section 1. Power of municipalities to amend their charters

Section 2. Construction of buildings for industrial use

Article IX: General Provisions – Page 70

Section 1. Oaths and subscriptions

Section 2. Offices incompatible with each other; election to Congress disqualifies

Section 3. Commissions

Section 4. Elections on the first Wednesday after first Tuesday of January may be adjourned from day to day

Section 5. Removal by impeachment or address

Section 6. Tenure of office

Section 7. Valuation

Section 8. Taxation

1. Intangible property
2. Assessment of certain lands based on current use; penalty on change to higher use
3. School districts
4. Watercraft
5. Historic and scenic preservation

Section 9. Power of taxation

Section 10. Tenure of sheriffs

Removal of sheriffs from office and replacement

Section 11. Attorney General

Section 12. Voting districts

Section 13. Bribery at elections

Section 14. Authority and procedure for issuance of bonds

Section 14-A. Authority to insure industrial, manufacturing, fishing, and agricultural mortgage loans

Section 14-B. Authority to insure revenue bonds of the Maine School Building Authority

Section 14-C. Authority to insure mortgage loans for Indian housing

Section 14-D. Authority to insure Maine veterans' mortgage loans, and to appropriate moneys and issue bonds for the payment of same

Section 15. Municipal borrowing regulated by Legislature through general law

Section 16. Seat of government

Section 17. Continuity of Government in case of enemy attack

Section 18. Limitation on use of funds of Maine State Retirement System

Section 18-A. Funding of retirement benefits under the Maine State Retirement System

Section 18-B. Payment of unfunded liabilities of the Maine State Retirement System

Section 19. Limitation on expenditure of motor vehicle and motor vehicle fuel revenues

Section 20. Mining Excise Tax Trust Fund

Section 21. State mandates

Section 22. Revenues generated by fisheries and wildlife management

Section 23. State park land

Section 24. Reapportionment

1. Procedure
2. Court apportionment
3. Judicial review

Section 25. Apportionment of county commissioner districts

1. Redistricting, generally
2. Supreme Judicial Court

Article X: Additional Provisions – Page 87

Section 1. (See Section 7 Note)

Section 2. (See Section 7 and Note)

Section 3. Laws now in force continue until repealed

Section 4. Amendments to Constitution

Section 5. (See Section 7 and Note)

Section 6. Constitution to be arranged by Chief Justice of the Supreme Judicial Court; Constitution to be enrolled and printed with laws; supreme law of the State

Section 7. Original sections 1, 2, 5, of Article X not to be printed; Section 5 in full force.

PREAMBLE

Objects of government. We the people of Maine, in order to establish justice, insure tranquility, provide for our mutual defense, promote our common welfare, and secure to ourselves and our posterity the blessings of liberty, acknowledging with grateful hearts the goodness of the Sovereign Ruler of the Universe in affording us an opportunity, so favorable to the design; and, imploring God's aid and direction in its accomplishment, do agree to form ourselves into a free and independent State, by the style and title of the State of Maine and do ordain and establish the following Constitution for the government of the same.

ARTICLE I: DECLARATION OF RIGHTS

Section 1. Natural rights

All people are born equally free and independent, and have certain natural, inherent and unalienable rights, among which are those of enjoying and defending life and liberty, acquiring, possessing and protecting property, and of pursuing and obtaining safety and happiness.

Section 2. Power inherent in people

All power is inherent in the people; all free governments are founded in their authority and instituted for their benefit; they have therefore an unalienable and indefeasible right to institute government, and to alter, reform, or totally change the same, when their safety and happiness require it.

Section 3. Religious freedom; sects equal; religious tests prohibited; religious teachers

All individuals have a natural and unalienable right to worship Almighty God according to the dictates of their own consciences, and no person shall be hurt, molested or restrained in that person's liberty or estate for worshipping God in the manner and season most agreeable to the dictates of that person's own conscience, nor for that person's religious professions or sentiments, provided that that person does not disturb the public peace, nor obstruct others in their religious worship; -- and all persons demeaning themselves peaceably, as good members of the State, shall be equally under the protection of the laws, and no subordination nor preference of any one sect or denomination to another shall ever be established by law, nor shall any religious test be required as a qualification for any office or trust, under this State; and all religious societies in this State, whether incorporate or unincorporate, shall at all times have the exclusive right of electing their public teachers, and contracting with them for their support and maintenance.

Section 4. Freedom of speech and publication; libel; truth given in evidence; jury determines law and fact

Every citizen may freely speak, write and publish sentiments on any subject, being responsible for the abuse of this liberty; no laws shall be passed regulating or restraining the freedom of the press; and in prosecutions for any publication respecting the official conduct of people in public capacity, or the qualifications of those who are candidates for the suffrages of the people, or where the matter published is proper for public information, the truth thereof may be given in evidence, and in all indictments for libels, the jury, after having received the direction of the court, shall have a right to determine, at their discretion, the law and the fact.

Section 5. Unreasonable searches prohibited

The people shall be secure in their persons, houses, papers and possessions from all unreasonable searches and seizures; and no warrant to search any place, or seize any person or thing, shall issue without a special designation of the place to be searched, and the person or thing to be seized, nor without probable cause -- supported by oath or affirmation.

Section 6. Rights of persons accused

In all criminal prosecutions, the accused shall have a right to be heard by the accused and counsel to the accused, or either, at the election of the accused;

To demand the nature and cause of the accusation, and have a copy thereof;

To be confronted by the witnesses against the accused;

To have compulsory process for obtaining witnesses in favor of the accused;

To have a speedy, public and impartial trial, and, except in trials by martial law or impeachment, by a jury of the vicinity. The accused shall not be compelled to furnish or give evidence against himself or herself, nor be deprived of life, liberty, property or privileges, but by judgment of that person's peers or the law of the land.

Section 6-A. Discrimination against persons prohibited

No person shall be deprived of life, liberty or property without due process of law, nor be denied the equal protection of the laws, nor be denied the enjoyment of that person's civil rights or be discriminated against in the exercise thereof.

Section 7. No person to answer to certain crimes but on indictment; exceptions; juries

No person shall be held to answer for a capital or infamous crime, unless on a presentment or indictment of a grand jury, except in cases of impeachment, or in such cases of offenses, as are usually cognizable by a justice of the peace, or in cases arising in the army or navy, or in the militia when in actual service in time of war or public danger. The Legislature shall provide by law a suitable and impartial mode of selecting juries, and their usual number and unanimity, in indictments and convictions, shall be held indispensable.

Section 8. No double jeopardy

No person, for the same offense, shall be twice put in jeopardy of life or limb.

Section 9. Sanguinary laws, excessive bail, cruel or unusual punishments prohibited

Sanguinary laws shall not be passed; all penalties and punishments shall be proportioned to the offense; excessive bail shall not be required, nor excessive fines imposed, nor cruel nor unusual punishments inflicted.

Section 10. Bailable offenses; habeas corpus

No person before conviction shall be bailable for any of the crimes which now are, or have been denominated capital offenses since the adoption of the Constitution, when the proof is evident or the presumption great, whatever the punishment of the crimes may be. And the privilege of the writ of habeas corpus shall not be suspended, unless when in cases of rebellion or invasion the public safety may require it.

Section 11. Attainder, ex post facto and contract-impairment laws prohibited

The Legislature shall pass no bill of attainder, ex post facto law, nor law impairing the obligation of contracts, and no attainder shall work corruption of blood nor forfeiture of estate.

Section 12. Treason; testimony of 2 witnesses

Treason against this State shall consist only in levying war against it, adhering to its enemies, giving them aid and comfort. No person shall be convicted of treason unless on the testimony of 2 witnesses to the same overt act, or confession in open court.

Section 13. Suspension of laws

The laws shall not be suspended but by the Legislature or its authority.

Section 14. Corporal punishment under military law

No person shall be subject to corporal punishment under military law, except such as are employed in the army or navy, or in the militia when in actual service in time of war or public danger.

Section 15. Right of petition

The people have a right at all times in an orderly and peaceable manner to assemble to consult upon the common good, to give instructions to their representatives, and to request, of either department of the government by petition or remonstrance, redress of their wrongs and grievances.

Section 16. To keep and bear arms

Every citizen has a right to keep and bear arms and this right shall never be questioned.

Section 17. Standing armies

No standing army shall be kept up in time of peace without the consent of the Legislature, and the military shall, in all cases, and at all times, be in strict subordination to the civil power.

Section 18. Quartering of soldiers on citizens

No soldier shall in time of peace be quartered in any house without the consent of the owner or occupant, nor in time of war, but in a manner to be prescribed by law.

Section 19. Right of redress for injuries

Every person, for an injury inflicted on the person or the person's reputation, property or immunities, shall have remedy by due course of law; and right and justice shall be administered freely and without sale, completely and without denial, promptly and without delay.

Section 20. Trial by jury

In all civil suits, and in all controversies concerning property, the parties shall have a right to a trial by jury, except in cases where it has heretofore been otherwise practiced; the party claiming the right may be heard by himself or herself and with counsel, or either, at the election of the party.

Section 21. Private property, when to be taken

Private property shall not be taken for public uses without just compensation; nor unless the public exigencies require it.

Section 22. Taxes

No tax or duty shall be imposed without the consent of the people or of their representatives in the Legislature.

Section 23. Title of nobility prohibited; tenure of offices

No title of nobility or hereditary distinction, privilege, honor or emolument, shall ever be granted or confirmed, nor shall any office be created, the appointment to which shall be for a longer time than during good behavior.

Section 24. Other rights not impaired

The enumeration of certain rights shall not impair nor deny others retained by the people.

ARTICLE II: ELECTORS

Section 1. Qualifications of electors; written ballot; military servicemen; students

Every citizen of the United States of the age of 18 years and upwards, excepting persons under guardianship for reasons of mental illness, having his or her residence established in this State, shall be an elector for Governor, Senators and Representatives, in the city, town or plantation where his or her residence has been established, if he or she continues to reside in this State; and the elections shall be by written ballot. But persons in the military, naval or marine service of the United States, or this State, shall not be considered as having obtained such established residence by being stationed in any garrison, barrack or military place, in any city, town or plantation; nor shall the residence of a student at any seminary of learning entitle the student to the right of suffrage in the city, town or plantation where such seminary is established. No person, however, shall be deemed to have lost residence by reason of the person's absence from the state in the military service of the United States, or of this State.

Indians. Every Indian, residing on tribal reservations and otherwise qualified, shall be an elector in all county, state and national elections.

Section 2. Electors exempt from arrests on election days

Electors shall, in all cases, except treason, felony or breach of the peace, be privileged from arrest on the days of election, during their attendance at, going to, and returning therefrom.

Section 3. Exemption from military duty

No elector shall be obliged to do duty in the militia on any day of election, except in time of war or public danger.

Section 4. Time of state election; absentee voting

The election of Senators and Representatives shall be on the Tuesday following the first Monday of November biennially forever and the election of Governor shall be on the Tuesday following the first Monday of November every 4 years. The Legislature under proper enactment shall authorize and provide for voting by citizens of the State absent therefrom in the Armed Forces of the United States or of this State and for voting by other citizens absent or physically incapacitated for reasons deemed sufficient.

Section 5. Voting machines

Voting machines, or other mechanical devices for voting, may be used at all elections under such regulations as may be prescribed by law, provided, however, the right of secret voting shall be preserved.

ARTICLE III: DISTRIBUTION OF POWERS

Section 1. Powers distributed

The powers of this government shall be divided into 3 distinct departments, the legislative, executive and judicial.

Section 2. To be kept separate

No person or persons, belonging to one of these departments, shall exercise any of the powers properly belonging to either of the others, except in the cases herein expressly directed or permitted.

ARTICLE IV: PART FIRST - HOUSE OF REPRESENTATIVES

Section 1. Legislative department; style of acts

The legislative power shall be vested in 2 distinct branches, a House of Representatives, and a Senate, each to have a negative on the other, and both to be styled the Legislature of Maine, but the people reserve to themselves power to propose laws and to enact or reject the same at the polls independent of the Legislature, and also reserve power at their own option to approve or reject at the polls any Act, bill, resolve or resolution passed by the joint action of both branches of the Legislature, and the style of their laws and Acts shall be, "Be it enacted by the people of the State of Maine."

Section 2. Number of Representatives; biennial terms; division of the State into districts for House of Representatives

The House of Representatives shall consist of 151 members, to be elected by the qualified electors, and hold their office 2 years from the day next preceding the first Wednesday in December following the general election. The Legislature which convenes in 2013, and also the Legislature which convenes in 2021 and every 10th year thereafter, shall cause the State to be divided into districts for the choice of one Representative for each district. The number of Representatives shall be divided into the number of inhabitants of the State exclusive of foreigners not naturalized according to the latest Federal Decennial Census or a State Census previously ordered by the Legislature to coincide with the Federal Decennial Census, to determine a mean population figure for each Representative District. Each Representative District shall be formed of contiguous and compact territory and shall cross political subdivision lines the least number of times necessary to establish as nearly as practicable equally populated districts. Whenever the population of a municipality entitles it to more than one district, all whole districts shall be drawn within municipal boundaries. Any population remainder within the municipality shall be included in a district with contiguous territory and shall be kept intact.

Section 3. Submission of reapportionment plan to Clerk of House; Legislature's action on commission's plan

The apportionment plan of the commission established under Article IV, Part Third, Section 1-A shall be submitted to the Clerk of the House no later than June 1st of the year in which apportionment is required. In the preparation of legislation implementing the plan, the commission, following a unanimous decision by commission members, may adjust errors and inconsistencies in accordance with the standards set forth in this Constitution, so long as substantive changes are not made. The Legislature shall enact the submitted plan of the commission or a plan of its own by a vote of 2/3 of the Members of each House by June 11th of the year in which apportionment is required. Such action shall be subject to the Governor's approval as provided in Article IV, Part Third, Section 2.

In the event that the Legislature shall fail to make an apportionment by June 11th, the Supreme Judicial Court shall, within 60 days following the period in which the Legislature is required to act, but fails to do so, make the apportionment. In making such apportionment, the Supreme Judicial Court shall take into consideration plans and briefs filed by the public with the court during the first 30 days of the period in which the court is required to apportion.

The Supreme Judicial Court shall have original jurisdiction to hear any challenge to an apportionment law enacted by the Legislature, as registered by any citizen or group thereof. If any challenge is sustained, the Supreme Judicial Court shall make the apportionment.

Section 4. Qualifications; residency requirement

No person shall be a member of the House of Representatives, unless the person shall, at the commencement of the period for which the person is elected, have been 5 years a citizen of the United States, have arrived at the age of 21 years, have been a resident in this State one year; and for the 3 months next preceding the time of this person's election shall have been, and, during the period for which elected, shall continue to be a resident in the district which that person represents.

No person may be a candidate for election as a member of the House of Representatives unless, at the time of the nomination for placement on a primary, general or special election ballot, that person is a resident in the district which the candidate seeks to represent.

Section 5. Election of Representatives; lists of votes delivered forthwith; lists of votes examined by Governor; summons of persons who appear to be elected; lists shall be laid before the House

The meetings within this State for the choice of Representatives shall be warned in due course of law by qualified officials of the several towns and cities 7 days at least before the election, and the election officials of the various towns and cities shall preside impartially at such meetings, receive the votes of all the qualified electors, sort, count and declare them in open meeting; and a list of the persons voted for shall be formed, with the number of votes for each person against that person's name. Cities and towns belonging to any Representative District shall hold their meetings at the same time in the respective cities and towns; and such meetings shall be notified, held and regulated, the votes received, sorted, counted and declared in the same manner. Fair copies of the lists of votes shall be attested by the municipal officers and the clerks of the cities and towns and the city and town clerks respectively shall cause the same to be delivered into the office of the Secretary of State forthwith. The Governor shall examine the returned copies of such lists and 7 days before the first

Wednesday of December biennially, shall issue a summons to such persons as shall appear to have been elected by a plurality of all votes returned, to attend and take their seats. All such lists shall be laid before the House of Representatives on the first Wednesday of December biennially, and they shall finally determine who are elected.

Section 6. Vacancies

Whenever the seat of a member shall be vacated by death, resignation, or otherwise the vacancy may be filled by a new election.

Section 7. To choose own officers

The House of Representatives shall choose their speaker, clerk and other officers.

Section 8. Power of impeachment

The House of Representatives shall have the sole power of impeachment.

ARTICLE IV: PART SECOND – SENATE

Section 1. Number of Senators

The Senate shall consist of an odd number of Senators, not less than 31 nor more than 35, elected at the same time and for the same term as Representatives by the qualified electors of the districts into which the State shall be from time to time divided.

Section 2. Submission of reapportionment plan to Secretary of Senate; Legislature's action on commission's plan; division of State into Senatorial Districts; division by Supreme Judicial Court

The Legislature which shall convene in the year 2013, and also the Legislature which shall convene in the year 2021 and every tenth year thereafter, shall cause the State to be divided into districts for the choice of a Senator from each district, using the same method as provided in Article IV, Part First, Section 2 for apportionment of Representative Districts.

The apportionment plan of the commission established under Article IV, Part Third, Section 1-A shall be submitted to the Secretary of the Senate no later than June 1st of the year in which apportionment is required. In the preparation of legislation implementing the plan, the commission, following a unanimous decision by commission members, may adjust errors and inconsistencies in accordance with the standards set forth in this Constitution, so long as substantive changes are not made. The Legislature shall enact the submitted plan of the commission or a plan of its own by a vote of 2/3 of the Members of each House by June 11th of the year in which apportionment is required. Such action shall be subject to the Governor's approval as provided in Article IV, Part Third, Section 2.

In the event that the Legislature shall fail to make an apportionment by June 11th, the Supreme Judicial Court shall, within 60 days following the period in which the Legislature is required to act but fails to do so, make the apportionment. In making such apportionment, the Supreme Judicial Court shall take into consideration plans and briefs filed by the public with the court during the first 30 days of the period in which the court is required to apportion.

The Supreme Judicial Court shall have original jurisdiction to hear any challenge to an apportionment law enacted by the Legislature, as registered by any citizen or group thereof. If any challenge is sustained, the Supreme Judicial Court shall make the apportionment.

Section 3. Election of Senators; lists of votes delivered forthwith

The meetings within this State for the election of Senators shall be notified, held and regulated and the votes received, sorted, counted, declared and recorded, in the same manner as those for Representatives. Fair copies of the lists of votes shall be attested by the clerks of the cities and towns or other duly authorized officials and sealed up in open meetings and such officials shall cause said lists to be delivered into the office of the Secretary of State forthwith.

Section 4. Lists of votes examined by Governor; summons to persons who appear to be elected

The Governor shall, as soon as may be, examine the copies of such lists, and at least 7 days before the said first Wednesday of December, issue a summons to such persons, as shall appear to be elected by a plurality of the votes in each senatorial district, to attend that day and take their seats.

Section 5. Determination of Senators elected; procedure for filling vacancies

The Senate shall, on said first Wednesday of December, biennially determine who is elected by a plurality of votes to be Senator in each district. All vacancies in the Senate arising from death, resignation, removal from the State or like causes, and also vacancies, if any, which may occur because of the failure of any district to elect by a plurality of votes the Senator to which said district shall be entitled shall be filled by an immediate election in the unrepresented district. The Governor shall issue a proclamation therefor and therein fix the time of such election.

Section 6. Qualifications

The Senators shall be 25 years of age at the commencement of the term, for which they are elected, and in all other respects their qualifications shall be the same as those of the Representatives.

Section 7. To try impeachments; limitation of judgment of impeachment; party liable to be tried and punished in court

The Senate shall have the sole power to try all impeachments, and when sitting for that purpose shall be on oath or affirmation, and no person shall be convicted without the concurrence of 2/3 of the members present. Their judgment, however, shall not extend farther than to removal from office, and disqualification to hold or enjoy any office of honor, trust or profit under this State. But the party, whether convicted or acquitted, shall nevertheless be liable to indictment, trial, judgment and punishment according to law.

Section 8. To choose own officers

The Senate shall choose their President, Secretary and other officers.

ARTICLE IV: PART THIRD - LEGISLATIVE POWER

Section 1. To meet annually; power of Legislature to convene itself at other times; extent of legislative power

The Legislature shall convene on the first Wednesday of December following the general election in what shall be designated the first regular session of the Legislature; and shall further convene on the first Wednesday after the first Tuesday of January in the subsequent even-numbered year in what shall be designated the second regular session of the Legislature; provided, however, that the business of the second regular session of the Legislature shall be limited to budgetary matters; legislation in the Governor's call; legislation of an emergency nature admitted by the Legislature; legislation referred to committees for study and report by the Legislature in the first regular session; and legislation presented to the Legislature by written petition of the electors under the provisions of Article IV, Part Third, Section 18. The Legislature shall enact appropriate statutory limits on the length of the first regular session and of the second regular session. The Legislature may convene at such other times on the call of the President of the Senate and Speaker of the House, with the consent of a majority of the Members of the Legislature of each political party, all Members of the Legislature having been first polled. The Legislature, with the exceptions hereinafter stated, shall have full power to make and establish all reasonable laws and regulations for the defense and benefit of the people of this State, not repugnant to this Constitution, nor to that of the United States.

Section 1-A. Legislature to establish Apportionment Commission; number of quorum; compensation of commission members; commission's budget; division among political parties

A Legislature which is required to apportion the districts of the House of Representatives or the Senate, or both, under Article IV, Part First, Section 2, or Article IV, Part Second, Section 2, shall establish, within the first 3 calendar days after the convening of that Legislature, a commission to develop in accordance with the requirements of this Constitution, a plan for apportioning the House of Representatives, the Senate, or both.
The commission shall be composed of 3 members from the political party holding the largest number of seats in the House of Representatives, who shall be appointed by the Speaker; 3 members from the political party holding the majority of the remainder of the seats in the House of Representatives, who shall be appointed by the floor leader of that party in the House; 2 members of the party holding the largest number of seats in the Senate, who shall be appointed by the President of the Senate; 2 members of the political party holding the majority of the remainder of the seats in the Senate, to be appointed by the floor leader of that party in the Senate; the chairperson of each of the 2 major political parties in the State or their designated representatives; and 3 members from the public generally, one to be selected by each group of members of the commission representing the same political party, and the third to be selected by the other 2 public members. The Speaker of the House shall be responsible for organizing the commission and shall be chairperson pro tempore thereof until a permanent chairperson is selected by the commission members from among their own number. No action may be taken without a quorum of 8 being present. The commission shall hold public hearings on any plan for apportionment prior to submitting such plan to the Legislature. Public members of the commission shall receive the same rate of per diem that is paid to Legislators for every day's attendance at

special sessions of the Legislature as defined by law. All members of the commission shall be reimbursed for actual travel expenses incurred in carrying out the business of the commission. The Legislature which is required to apportion shall establish a budget for the apportioning commission within the state budget document in the fiscal year previous to the fiscal year during which the apportioning commission is required to convene and shall appropriate sufficient funds for the commission to satisfactorily perform its duties and responsibilities. The budget shall include sufficient funds to compensate the chairperson of the commission and the chairperson's staff. The remainder of the appropriation shall be made available equally among the political parties represented on the commission to provide travel expenses, incidental expenses and compensation for commission members and for partisan staff and operations.

Section 2. Bills to be signed by the Governor; proceedings, in case the Governor disapproves; allowing the Governor 10 days to act on legislation

Every bill or resolution, having the force of law, to which the concurrence of both Houses may be necessary, except on a question of adjournment, which shall have passed both Houses, shall be presented to the Governor, and if the Governor approves, the Governor shall sign it; if not, the Governor shall return it with objections to the House in which it shall have originated, which shall enter the objections at large on its journals, and proceed to reconsider it. If after such reconsideration, 2/3 of that House shall agree to pass it, it shall be sent together with the objections, to the other House, by which it shall be reconsidered, and, if approved by 2/3 of that House, it shall have the same effect as if it had been signed by the Governor; but in all such cases, the votes of both Houses shall be taken by yeas and nays, and the names of the persons, voting for and against the bill or resolution, shall be entered on the journals of both Houses respectively. If the bill or resolution shall not be returned by the Governor within 10 days

(Sundays excepted) after it shall have been presented to the Governor, it shall have the same force and effect as if the Governor had signed it unless the Legislature by their adjournment prevent its return, in which case it shall have such force and effect, unless returned within 3 days after the next meeting of the same Legislature which enacted the bill or resolution; if there is no such next meeting of the Legislature which enacted the bill or resolution, the bill or resolution shall not be a law.

Section 2-A. Line-item veto of dollar amounts appearing in appropriation or allocation sections of legislative documents

The Governor has power to disapprove any dollar amount appearing in an appropriation section or allocation section, or both, of an enacted legislative document. Unless the Governor exercises the line-item veto power authorized in this section no later than one day after receiving for signature the enacted legislation, the powers of the Governor as set out in Section 2 apply to the entire enacted legislation. For any disapproved dollar amount, the Governor shall replace the dollar amount with one that does not result in an increase in an appropriation or allocation or a decrease in a deappropriation or deallocation. When disapproving a dollar amount pursuant to this section, the Governor may not propose an increase in an appropriation or allocation elsewhere in the legislative document. The Governor shall specify the distinct dollar amounts that are revised, and the part or parts of the legislative document not specifically revised become law. The dollar amounts in an appropriation or allocation that have been disapproved become law as revised by the Governor, unless passed over the Governor's veto by the Legislature as the dollar amounts originally appeared in the enacted bill as presented to the Governor; except that, notwithstanding any other provision of this Constitution for dollar amounts vetoed pursuant to this section, a majority of all the elected members in each House is sufficient to override the veto, and each dollar amount vetoed must be voted on separately to override the veto. Except as provided in this section, the Governor may not disapprove, omit or modify any language allocated to the statutes or appearing in an unallocated section of law.

Section 3. Each House the judge of its elections; majority, a quorum

Each House shall be the judge of the elections and qualifications of its own members, and a majority shall constitute a quorum to do business; but a smaller number may adjourn from day to day, and may compel the attendance of absent members, in such manner and under such penalties as each House shall provide.

Section 4. May punish and expel members

Each House may determine the rules of its proceedings, punish its members for disorderly behavior, and, with the concurrence of 2/3, expel a member, but not a 2nd time for the same cause.

Section 5. Shall keep a journal; yeas and nays

Each House shall keep a journal, and from time to time publish its proceedings, except such parts as in their judgment may require secrecy; and the yeas and nays of the members of either House on any question, shall, at the desire of 1/5 of those present, be entered on the journals.

Section 6. May punish for contempt

Each House, during its session, may punish by imprisonment any person, not a member, for disrespectful or disorderly behavior in its presence, for obstructing any of its proceedings, threatening, assaulting or abusing any of its members for anything said, done, or doing in either House; provided, that no imprisonment shall extend beyond the period of the same session.

Section 7. Compensation; traveling expenses

The Senators and Representatives shall receive such compensation, as shall be established by law; but no law increasing their compensation shall take effect during the existence of the Legislature, which enacted it. The expenses of the members of the House of Representatives in traveling to the Legislature, and returning therefrom, once in each week of each session and no more, shall be paid by the State out of the public treasury to every member, who shall seasonably attend, in the judgment of the House, and does not depart therefrom without leave.

Section 8. Members exempt from arrest; freedom of debate

The Senators and Representatives shall, in all cases except treason, felony or breach of the peace, be privileged from arrest during their attendance at, going to, and returning from each session of the Legislature, and no member shall be liable to answer for anything spoken in debate in either House, in any court or place elsewhere.

Section 9. Either House may originate bills; revenue bills

Bills, orders or resolutions, may originate in either House, and may be altered, amended or rejected in the other; but all bills for raising a revenue shall originate in the House of Representatives, but the Senate may propose amendments as in other cases; provided, that they shall not, under color of amendment, introduce any new matter, which does not relate to raising a revenue.

Section 10. Members not to be appointed to certain offices

No Senator or Representative shall, during the term for which the Senator or Representative shall have been elected, be appointed to any civil office of profit under this State, which requires the approval of the Legislature for appointment or which shall have been created, or the emoluments of which increased during such term, except such offices as may be filled by elections by the people.

Section 11. Persons disqualified to be members

No member of Congress, nor person holding any office under the United States (post officers excepted) nor office of profit under this State, justices of the peace, notaries public, coroners and officers of the militia excepted, shall have a seat in either House while a member of Congress, or continuing in such office.

Section 12. Adjournments

Neither House shall during the session, without the consent of the other, adjourn for more than 2 days, nor to any other place than that in which the Houses shall be sitting.

Section 13. Special legislation

The Legislature shall, from time to time, provide, as far as practicable, by general laws, for all matters usually appertaining to special or private legislation.

Section 14. Corporations, formed under general laws

Corporations shall be formed under general laws, and shall not be created by special Acts of the Legislature, except for municipal purposes, and in cases where the objects of the corporation cannot otherwise be attained; and, however formed, they shall forever be subject to the general laws of the State.

Section 15. Constitutional conventions

The Legislature shall, by a 2/3 concurrent vote of both branches, have the power to call constitutional conventions, for the purpose of amending this Constitution.

Section 16. Acts become effective in 90 days after recess; exception; emergency bill defined

No Act or joint resolution of the Legislature, except such orders or resolutions as pertain solely to facilitating the performance of the business of the Legislature, of either branch, or of any committee or officer thereof, or appropriate money therefor or for the payment of salaries fixed by law, shall take effect until 90 days after the recess of the session of the Legislature in which it was passed, unless in case of emergency, which with the facts constituting the emergency shall be expressed in the preamble of the Act, the Legislature shall, by a vote of 2/3 of all the members elected to each House, otherwise direct. An emergency bill shall include only such measures as are immediately necessary for the preservation of the public peace, health or safety; and shall not include (1) an infringement of the right of home rule for municipalities, (2) a franchise or a license to a corporation or an individual to extend longer than one year, or (3) provision for the sale or purchase or renting for more than 5 years of real estate.

Section 17. Proceedings for people's veto

1. Petition procedure; petition for people's veto

Upon written petition of electors, the number of which shall not be less than 10% of the total vote for Governor cast in the last gubernatorial election preceding the filing of such petition, and addressed to the Governor and filed in the office of the Secretary of State by the hour of 5:00 pm., on or before the 90th day after the recess of the Legislature, or if such 90th day is a Saturday, a Sunday, or a legal holiday, by the hour of 5:00 pm., on the preceding day which is not a Saturday, a Sunday, or a legal holiday, requesting that one or more Acts, bills, resolves or resolutions, or part or parts thereof, passed by the Legislature but not then in effect by reason of the provisions of the preceding section, be referred to the people, such Acts, bills, resolves, or resolutions or part or parts thereof as are specified in such petition shall not take effect until 30 days after the Governor shall have announced by public proclamation that the same have been ratified by a majority of the electors voting thereon at a statewide or general election.

2. Effect of referendum

The effect of any Act, bill, resolve or resolution or part or parts thereof as are specified in such petition shall be suspended upon the filing of such petition. If it is later finally determined, in accordance with any procedure enacted by the Legislature pursuant to the Constitution, that such petition was invalid, such Act, bill, resolve or resolution or part or parts thereof shall then take effect upon the day following such final determination.

3. Referral to electors; proclamation by Governor

As soon as it appears that the effect of any Act, bill, resolve, or resolution or part or parts thereof has been suspended by petition in manner aforesaid, the Governor by public proclamation shall give notice thereof and of the time when such measure is to be voted on by the people, which shall be at the next statewide or general election, whichever comes first, not less than 60 days after such proclamation. If the Governor fails to order such measure to be submitted to the people at the next statewide or general election, the Secretary of State shall, by proclamation, order such measure to be submitted to the people at such an election and such order shall be sufficient to enable the people to vote.

Section 18. Direct initiative of legislation

1. Petition procedure

The electors may propose to the Legislature for its consideration any bill, resolve or resolution, including bills to amend or repeal emergency legislation but not an amendment of the State Constitution, by written petition addressed to the Legislature or to either branch thereof and filed in the office of the Secretary of State by the hour of 5:00 p.m., on or before the 50th day after the date of convening of the Legislature in first regular session or on or before the 25th day after the date of convening of the Legislature in second regular session, except that the written petition may not be filed in the office of the Secretary of State later than 18 months after the date the petition form was furnished or approved by the Secretary of State. If the applicable deadline falls on a Saturday, Sunday, or legal holiday, the period runs until the hour of 5:00 pm., of the next day which is not a Saturday, Sunday, or legal holiday.

2. Referral to electors unless enacted by the Legislature without change; number of signatures necessary on direct initiative petitions; dating signatures on petitions; competing measures

For any measure thus proposed by electors, the number of signatures shall not be less than 10% of the total vote for Governor cast in the last gubernatorial election preceding the filing of such petition. The date each signature was made shall be written next to the signature on the petition. A signature is not valid if it is dated more than one year prior to the date that the petition was filed in the office of the Secretary of State. The measure thus proposed, unless enacted without change by the

Legislature at the session at which it is presented, shall be submitted to the electors together with any amended form, substitute, or recommendation of the Legislature, and in such manner that the people can choose between the competing measures or reject both. When there are competing bills and neither receives a majority of the votes given for or against both, the one receiving the most votes shall at the next statewide election to be held not less than 60 days after the first vote thereon be submitted by itself if it receives more than 1/3 of the votes given for and against both. If the measure initiated is enacted by the Legislature without change, it shall not go to a referendum vote unless in pursuance of a demand made in accordance with the preceding section. The Legislature may order a special election on any measure that is subject to a vote of the people.

3. Timing of elections; proclamation by Governor

The Governor shall, by proclamation, order any measure proposed to the Legislature as herein provided, and not enacted by the Legislature without change, referred to the people at an election to be held in November of the year in which the petition is filed. If the Governor fails to order a measure proposed to the Legislature and not enacted without change to be submitted to the people at such an election by proclamation within 10 days after the recess of the Legislature to which the measure was proposed, the Secretary of State shall, by proclamation, order such measure to be submitted to the people at an election as requested, and such order shall be sufficient to enable the people to vote.

Section 19. Effective date of measures approved by people; veto power limited

Any measure referred to the people and approved by a majority of the votes given thereon shall, unless a later date is specified in said measure, take effect and become a law in 30 days after the

Governor has made public proclamation of the result of the vote on said measure, which the Governor shall do within 10 days after the vote thereon has been canvassed and determined; provided, however, that any such measure which entails expenditure in an amount in excess of available and unappropriated state funds shall remain inoperative until 45 days after the next convening of the Legislature in regular session, unless the measure provides for raising new revenues adequate for its operation. The veto power of the Governor shall not extend to any measure approved by vote of the people, and any measure initiated by the people and passed by the Legislature without change, if vetoed by the Governor and if the veto is sustained by the Legislature shall be referred to the people to be voted on at the next general election. The Legislature may enact measures expressly conditioned upon the people's ratification by a referendum vote.

Section 20. Meaning of words "electors," "people," "recess of Legislature," "statewide election," "measure," "circulator," and "written petition"; written petitions for people's veto; written petitions for direct initiative

As used in any of the 3 preceding sections or in this section the words "electors" and "people" mean the electors of the State qualified to vote for Governor; "recess of the Legislature" means the adjournment without day of a session of the Legislature; "statewide election" means any election held throughout the State on a particular day; "measure" means an Act, bill, resolve or resolution proposed by the people, or 2 or more such, or part or parts of such, as the case may be; "circulator" means a person who solicits signatures for written petitions, and who must be a resident of this State and whose name must appear on the voting list of the city, town or plantation of the circulator's residence as qualified to vote for Governor; "written petition" means one or more petitions written or printed, or partly written and partly printed, with the original signatures of the petitioners attached, verified as to the authenticity of the signatures by the oath of the circulator that all of the signatures to the petition were made in the presence of the circulator and that to the best of the circulator's knowledge and belief each signature is the signature of the person whose name it purports to be, and accompanied by the certificate of the official authorized by law to maintain the voting list or to certify signatures on petitions for voters on the voting list of the city, town or plantation in which the petitioners reside that their names appear on the voting list of the city, town or plantation of the official as qualified to vote for Governor. The oath of the circulator must be sworn to in the presence of a person authorized by law to administer oaths. Written petitions for a people's veto pursuant to Article IV, Part Third, Section 17 must be submitted to the appropriate officials of cities, towns or plantations, or state election officials as authorized by law, for determination of whether the petitioners are qualified voters by the hour of 5:00 pm., on the 5th day before the petition must be filed in the office of the Secretary of State, or, if such 5th day is a Saturday, a Sunday or a legal holiday, by 5:00 p.m., on the next day which is not a Saturday, a Sunday or a legal holiday. Written petitions for a direct initiative pursuant to Article IV, Part Third, Section 18 must be submitted to the appropriate officials of cities, towns or plantations, or state election officials as authorized by law, for determination of whether the petitioners are qualified voters by the hour of 5:00 p.m., on the 10th day before the petition must be filed in the office of the Secretary of State, or, if such 10th day is a Saturday, a Sunday or a legal holiday, by 5:00 pm., on the next day which is not a Saturday, a Sunday or a legal holiday. Such officials must complete the certification of only those petitions submitted by these deadlines and must return them to the circulators or their agents within 2 days for a petition for a people's veto and within 5 days for a petition for a direct initiative, Saturdays, Sundays and legal holidays excepted, of the date on which such petitions were submitted to them. Signatures on petitions not submitted to the appropriate local or state officials by these deadlines may not be certified. The petition shall set forth the full text of the measure requested or proposed.

Petition forms shall be furnished or approved by the Secretary of State upon written application signed and notarized and submitted to the office of the Secretary of State by a resident of this State whose name must appear on the voting list of the city, town or plantation of that resident as qualified to vote for Governor. The full text of a measure submitted to a vote of the people under the provisions of the Constitution need not be printed on the official ballots, but, until otherwise provided by the Legislature, the Secretary of State shall prepare the ballots in such form as to present the question or questions concisely and intelligibly.

Section 21. City council of any city may establish direct initiative and people's veto

The city council of any city may establish the direct initiative and people's veto for the electors of such city in regard to its municipal affairs, provided that the ordinance establishing and providing the method of exercising such direct initiative and people's veto shall not take effect until ratified by vote of a majority of the electors of said city, voting thereon at a municipal election. Provided, however, that the Legislature may at any time provide a uniform method for the exercise of the initiative and referendum in municipal affairs.

Section 22. Election officers and officials, how governed

Until the Legislature shall enact further laws not inconsistent with the Constitution for applying the people's veto and direct initiative, the election officers and other officials shall be governed by the provisions of this Constitution and of the general law, supplemented by such reasonable action as may be necessary to render the preceding sections self executing. The Legislature may enact laws not inconsistent with the Constitution to establish procedures for determination of the validity of written petitions. Such laws shall include provision for judicial review of any determination, to be completed within 100 days from the date of filing of a written petition in the office of the Secretary of State.

Section 23. Municipalities reimbursed annually

The Legislature shall annually reimburse each municipality from state tax sources for not less than 50% of the property tax revenue loss suffered by that municipality during the previous calendar year because of the statutory property tax exemptions or credits enacted after April 1, 1978. The Legislature shall enact appropriate legislation to carry out the intent of this section. This section shall allow, but not require, reimbursement for statutory property tax exemptions or credits for unextracted minerals.

ARTICLE V: PART FIRST - EXECUTIVE POWER

Section 1. Governor

The supreme executive power of this State shall be vested in a Governor.

Section 2. Term of office; reelection eligibility

The Governor shall be elected by the qualified electors, and shall hold the office for 4 years from the first Wednesday after the first Tuesday of January next following the election and until the successor to the Governor has been duly elected and qualified. The person who has served 2 consecutive popular elective 4-year terms of office as Governor shall be ineligible to succeed himself or herself.

Section 3. Election; votes to be returned to Secretary of State; Secretary of State to lay lists before the Senate and House of Representatives; provision in case of tie

The meetings for election of Governor shall be notified, held and regulated and votes shall be received, sorted, counted and declared and recorded, in the same manner as those for Senators and Representatives. Copies of lists of votes shall be sealed and returned to the secretary's office in the same manner and at the same time as those for Senators. The Secretary of State for the time being shall, on the first Wednesday after the first Tuesday of January then next, lay the lists returned to the secretary's office before the Senate and House of Representatives to be by them examined, together with the ballots cast if they so elect, and they shall determine the number of votes duly cast for the office of Governor, and in case of a choice by plurality of all of the votes returned they shall declare and publish the same. If there shall be a tie between the 2 persons having the largest number of votes for Governor, the House of Representatives and the Senate meeting in joint session, and each member of said bodies having a single vote, shall elect one of said 2 persons having so received an equal number of votes and the person so elected by the Senate and House of Representatives shall be declared the Governor.

Section 4. Qualifications

The Governor shall, at the commencement of the Governor's term, be not less than 30 years of age; a citizen of the United States for at least 15 years, have been 5 years a resident of the State; and at the time of election and during the term for which elected, be a resident of said State.

Section 5. Disqualifications

No person holding any office or place under the United States, this State, or any other power, shall assume the office of Governor, nor shall any such person exercise the office of Governor except as provided by this Constitution.

Section 6. Compensation

The Governor shall, at stated times, receive for services a compensation, which shall not be increased or diminished during the Governor's continuance in office.

Section 7. Commander in chief

The Governor shall be commander in chief of the army and navy of the State, and of the militia, except when the same are called into the actual service of the United States.

Section 8. To appoint officers

The Governor shall nominate, and, subject to confirmation as provided herein, appoint all judicial officers, except judges of probate and justices of the peace if their manner of selection is otherwise provided for by this Constitution or by law, and all other civil and military officers whose appointment is not by this Constitution, or shall not by law be otherwise provided for. Procedure for confirmation. The procedure for confirmation shall be as follows: an appropriate legislative committee comprised of members of both houses in reasonable proportion to their membership as provided by law shall recommend confirmation or denial by majority vote of committee members present and voting. The committee recommendation shall be reviewed by the Senate and upon review shall become final action of confirmation or denial unless the Senate by vote of 2/3 of those members present and voting overrides the committee recommendation. The Senate vote shall be by the yeas and nays.

Affirmative vote of 2/3 of members required

All statutes enacted to carry out the purposes of the second paragraph of this section shall require the affirmative vote of 2/3 of the members of each House present and voting.

Governor or President of Senate may call Senate into session

Either the Governor or the President of the Senate shall have the power to call the Senate into session for the purpose of voting upon confirmation of appointments.

Nomination by Governor made 7 days prior to appointment of nominee

Every nomination by the Governor shall be made 7 days at least prior to appointment of the nominee.

Section 9. To give information and recommend measures

The Governor shall from time to time give the Legislature information of the condition of the State, and recommend to their consideration such measures, as the Governor may judge expedient.

Section 10. May require information of any officer

The Governor may require information from any military officer, or any officer in the executive department, upon any subject relating to the duties of their respective offices.

Section 11. Power to pardon and remit penalties, etc.; conditions

The Governor shall have power to remit after conviction all forfeitures and penalties, and to grant reprieves, commutations and pardons, except in cases of impeachment, upon such conditions, and with such restrictions and limitations as may be deemed proper, subject to such regulations as may be provided by law, relative to the manner of applying for pardons. Such power to grant reprieves, commutations and pardons shall include offenses of juvenile delinquency.

Section 12. Shall enforce the laws

The Governor shall take care that the laws be faithfully executed.

Section 13. Convene the Legislature on extraordinary occasions, and adjourn it in case of disagreement; may change the place of meeting

The Governor may, on extraordinary occasions, convene the Legislature; and in case of disagreement between the 2 Houses with respect to the time of adjournment, adjourn them to such time, as the Governor shall think proper, not beyond the day of the next regular session; and if, since the last adjournment, the place where the Legislature were next to convene shall have become dangerous from an enemy or contagious sickness, may direct the session to be held at some other convenient place within the State.

Section 14. Vacancy, how supplied

Whenever the office of Governor shall become vacant because of the death, resignation or removal of a Governor in office, or any other cause, the President of the Senate shall assume the office of Governor until another Governor shall be duly qualified. When the vacancy occurs more than 90 days preceding the date of the primary election for nominating candidates to be voted for at the biennial election next succeeding, the President of the Senate shall assume the office of Governor until the first Wednesday after the first Tuesday of January following the biennial election. At the biennial election, a Governor shall be elected to fill the unexpired term created by the vacancy. When the vacancy occurs less than 90 days preceding the date of a primary election the President of the Senate shall fill the unexpired term.
Whenever the offices of Governor, and President of the Senate are vacant at the same time, the Speaker of the House of Representatives shall assume the office of Governor for the same term and under the same conditions as the President of the Senate. Whenever the offices of Governor, President of the Senate and Speaker of the House of Representatives are vacant at the same time, the person acting as Secretary of State for the time being shall exercise the office of Governor and shall forthwith by proclamation convene the Senate and the House of Representatives which shall fill respectively the vacancies in the offices of the President of the Senate and the Speaker of the House, and by joint ballot of the Senators and Representatives in convention choose a person who shall assume the office of Governor for the same term and under the same conditions as the

President of the Senate.

Mental or physical disability of the Governor continuously for more than 6 months. Whenever for 6 months a Governor in office shall have been continuously unable to discharge the powers and duties of that office because of mental or physical disability such office shall be deemed vacant. Such vacancy shall be declared by the Supreme Judicial Court upon presentment to it of a joint resolution declaring the ground of the vacancy, adopted by a vote of 2/3 of the Senators and Representatives in convention, and upon notice, hearing before the court and a decision by a majority of the court that ground exists for declaring the office to be vacant.

Section 15. Temporary mental or physical disability of Governor

Whenever the Governor is unable to discharge the powers and duties of that office because of mental or physical disability, the President of the Senate, or if that office is vacant, the Speaker of the House of Representatives, shall exercise the powers and duties of the office of Governor until the Governor is again able to discharge the powers and duties of that office, or until the office of Governor is declared to be vacant or until another Governor shall be duly qualified.

Whenever the Governor is unable to discharge the powers and duties of that office, the Governor may so certify to the Chief Justice of the Supreme Judicial Court, in which case and upon notice from the Chief Justice, the President of the Senate, or if that office is vacant, the Speaker of the House of Representatives, shall exercise the powers and duties of the office of Governor until such time as the Governor shall certify to the Chief Justice that the Governor is able to discharge such powers and duties and the Chief Justice shall so notify the officer who is exercising the powers and duties of the office of Governor.

When the Secretary of State shall have reason to believe that the Governor is unable to discharge the duties of that office, the Secretary of State may so certify to the Supreme Judicial Court, declaring the reason for such belief. After notice to the Governor, a hearing before the court and a decision by a majority of the court that the Governor is unable to discharge the duties of the office of Governor, the court shall notify the President of the Senate, or if that office is vacant the Speaker of the House of Representatives, of such inability and that officer shall exercise the functions, powers and duties of the office of Governor until such time as the Secretary of State or the Governor shall certify to the court that the Governor is able to discharge the duties of the office of Governor and the court, after notice to the Governor and a hearing before the court, decides that the Governor is able to discharge the duties of that office and so notifies the officer who is exercising the powers and duties of the office of Governor. Whenever either the President of the Senate or Speaker of the House of Representatives shall exercise the office of Governor, the officer shall receive only the compensation of Governor, but the officer's duties as President or Speaker shall be suspended; and the Senate or House shall fill the vacancy resulting from such suspension, until the officer shall cease to exercise the office of Governor.

ARTICLE V: PART SECOND – SECRETARY

Section 1. Election

The Secretary of State shall be chosen biennially at the first session of the Legislature, by joint ballot of the Senators and Representatives in convention.

Section 1-A. Succession to the office of Secretary of State

If a vacancy occurs in the office of the Secretary of State, the first deputy secretary of state shall act as the Secretary of State until a Secretary of State is elected by the Legislature during the current session if in session, or at the next regular or special session.

Section 2. Records of State; deputies

The records of the State shall be kept in the office of the secretary, who may appoint deputies to that office, for whose conduct the secretary shall be accountable.

Section 3. Attend the Governor, Senate, and House

The Secretary of State shall attend the Governor, Senate and House of Representatives, in person or by the deputies of the Secretary of State as they shall respectively require.
Section 4. Records of executive and legislative departments. The Secretary of State shall carefully keep and preserve the records of all the official acts and proceedings of the Governor, Senate and House of Representatives, and, when required, lay the same before either branch of the Legislature, and perform such other duties as are enjoined by this Constitution, or shall be required by law.

ARTICLE V: PART THIRD - TREASURER

Section 1. Election

The Treasurer shall be chosen biennially, at the first session of the Legislature, by joint ballot of the Senators, and Representatives in convention.

Section 1-A. Succession to the office of Treasurer

If a vacancy occurs in the office of Treasurer of State, the deputy treasurer of state shall act as the Treasurer of State until a Treasurer of State is elected by the Legislature during the current session if in session, or at the next regular or special session.

Section 2. Bond

The Treasurer shall, before entering on the duties of that office, give bond to the State with sureties, to the satisfaction of the Legislature, for the faithful discharge of that trust.

Section 3. Not to engage in trade

The Treasurer shall not, during the treasurer's continuance in office, engage in any business of trade or commerce, or as a broker, nor as an agent or factor for any merchant or trader.

Section 4. No money drawn except upon appropriation or allocation

No money shall be drawn from the treasury, except in consequence of appropriations or allocations authorized by law.

Section 5. Bonding regulations; prohibiting use of proceeds from sale of bonds to fund current expenditures

The Legislature shall enact general law prohibiting the use of proceeds from the sale of bonds to fund current expenditures and shall provide by appropriation for the payment of interest upon and installments of principal of all bonded debt created on behalf of the State as the same shall become due and payable. If at any time the Legislature shall fail to make any such appropriation, the Treasurer of State shall set apart from the first General Fund revenues thereafter received a sum sufficient to pay such interest or installments of principal and shall so apply the moneys thus set apart. The Treasurer of State may be required to set apart and apply such revenues at the suit of any holder of such bonds. The prohibition on use of proceeds from the sale of bonds to fund current expenditures shall only apply to those bonds authorized on or after July 1, 1977.

ARTICLE VI: JUDICIAL POWER

Section 1. Courts

The judicial power of this State shall be vested in a Supreme Judicial Court, and such other courts as the Legislature shall from time to time establish.

Section 2. Compensation

The Justices of the Supreme Judicial Court and the Judges of other courts shall, at stated times receive a compensation, which shall not be diminished during their continuance in office; but they shall receive no other fee or reward for their services as Justices or Judges.

Section 3. To give opinion when required by Governor or either Branch of the Legislature

The Justices of the Supreme Judicial Court shall be obliged to give their opinion upon important questions of law, and upon solemn occasions, when required by the Governor, Senate or House of Representatives.

Section 4. Tenure of judicial officers; 6-month holdover period

All judicial officers appointed by the Governor shall hold their offices for the term of 7 years from the time of their respective appointments (unless sooner removed by impeachment or by address of both branches of the Legislature to the executive, provided further that justices of the peace may be removed from office in such manner as the Legislature may provide); provided, however, that a judicial officer whose term of office has expired or who has reached mandatory retirement age, as provided by statute, may continue to hold office until the expiration of an additional period not to exceed 6 months or until the successor to the judicial officer is appointed, whichever occurs first in time.

Section 5. Limitation on holding other office

No Justice of the Supreme Judicial Court or any other court shall hold office under the United States or any other state, nor under this State, except as justice of the peace or as member of the Judicial Council.

Section 6. Judges and registers of probate, election and tenure; vacancies / Repealed.

Judges and registers of probate shall be elected by the people of their respective counties, by a plurality of the votes given in, at the biennial election on the Tuesday following the first Monday of November, and shall hold their offices for 4 years, commencing on the first day of January next after their election. Vacancies occurring in said offices by death, resignation or otherwise, shall be filled by election in manner aforesaid at the November election, next after their occurrence; and in the meantime, the Governor may fill said vacancies by appointment, and the persons so appointed shall hold their offices until the first day of January next after the election aforesaid.

ARTICLE VII: MILITARY

Section 1. Officers, how appointed

All commissioned officers of the militia shall be appointed and commissioned by the Governor, from such persons as are qualified by law to hold such offices.

Section 2. Qualifications and selection

The Legislature shall, by law, designate the qualifications necessary for holding a commission in the militia and shall prescribe the mode of selection of officers for the several grades.

Section 3. Adjutant General

The Adjutant General shall be appointed by the Governor. But the Adjutant General shall also perform the duties of quartermaster general and paymaster general until otherwise directed by law.

Section 4. Standard of organization, armament and discipline

The organization, armament and discipline of the militia and of the military and naval units thereof shall be the same as that which is now or may hereafter be prescribed by the laws and regulations of the United States; and it shall be the duty of the Governor to issue from time to time such orders and regulations and to adopt such other means of administration, as shall maintain the prescribed standard of organization, armament and discipline; and such orders, regulations and means adopted shall have the full force and effect of the law.

Section 5. Persons exempt from military duty

Persons of the denominations of Quakers and Shakers, Justices of the Supreme Judicial Court, Ministers of the Gospel and persons exempted by the laws of the United States may be exempted from military duty, but no other able-bodied person of the age of 18 and under the age of 45 years, excepting officers of the militia who have been honorably discharged, shall be so exempted.

ARTICLE VIII: PART FIRST – EDUCATION

Section 1. Legislature shall require towns to support public schools; duty of Legislature

A general diffusion of the advantages of education being essential to the preservation of the rights and liberties of the people; to promote this important object, the Legislature are authorized, and it shall be their duty to require, the several towns to make suitable provision, at their own expense, for the support and maintenance of public schools; and it shall further be their duty to encourage and suitably endow, from time to time, as the circumstances of the people may authorize, all academies, colleges and seminaries of learning within the State; provided, that no donation, grant or endowment shall at any time be made by the Legislature to any literary institution now established, or which may hereafter be established, unless, at the time of making such endowment, the Legislature of the State shall have the right to grant any further powers to alter, limit or restrain any of the powers vested in any such literary institution, as shall be judged necessary to promote the best interests thereof.

Section 2. Authority to pledge the credit of the State and to issue bonds for loans to Maine students in higher education and their parents

For the purpose of assisting the youth of Maine to achieve the required levels of learning and to develop their intellectual and mental capacities, the Legislature, by proper enactment, may authorize the credit of the State to be loaned to secure funds for loans to Maine students attending institutions of higher education, wherever situated, and to parents of these students. Funds shall be obtained by the issuance of state bonds, when authorized by the Governor, but the amount of bonds issued and outstanding shall not at one time exceed in the aggregate $4,000,000. Funds loaned shall be on such terms and conditions as the Legislature shall authorize.

ARTICLE VIII: PART SECOND - MUNICIPAL HOME RULE

Section 1. Power of municipalities to amend their charters

The inhabitants of any municipality shall have the power to alter and amend their charters on all matters, not prohibited by Constitution or general law, which are local and municipal in character. The Legislature shall prescribe the procedure by which the municipality may so act.

Section 2. Construction of buildings for industrial use

For the purposes of fostering, encouraging and assisting the physical location, settlement and resettlement of industrial and manufacturing enterprises within the physical boundaries of any municipality, the registered voters of that municipality may, by majority vote, authorize the issuance of notes or bonds in the name of the municipality for the purpose of purchasing land and interests therein or constructing buildings for industrial use, to be leased or sold by the municipality to any responsible industrial firm or corporation.

ARTICLE IX: GENERAL PROVISIONS

Section 1. Oaths and subscriptions

Every person elected or appointed to either of the places or offices provided in this Constitution, and every person elected, appointed, or commissioned to any judicial, executive, military or other office under this State, shall, before entering on the discharge of the duties of that place or office, take and subscribe the following oath or affirmation:

"I,   do swear, that I will support the Constitution of the United States and of this State, so long as I shall continue a citizen thereof. So help me God."

"I   do swear, that I will faithfully discharge, to the best of my abilities, the duties incumbent on me as   according to the Constitution and laws of the State. So help me God."

Alternative affirmation. Provided, that an affirmation in the above forms may be substituted, when the person shall be conscientiously scrupulous of taking and subscribing an oath. Administration of oaths to Governor, Senators, Representatives, and other officers. The oaths or affirmations shall be taken and subscribed by the Governor before the presiding officer of the Senate, in the presence of both Houses of the Legislature, and by the Senators and Representatives before the Governor, and by the residue of said officers before such persons as shall be prescribed by the Legislature; and whenever the Governor shall not be able to attend during the session of the Legislature to take and subscribe said oaths or affirmations, such oaths or affirmations may be taken and subscribed in the recess of the Legislature before any Justice of the Supreme Judicial Court and provided further that, if the Governor shall be unable to appear and administer the oath to the Senators and Representatives, such oaths shall be administered by the Chief Justice of the Supreme

Judicial Court or in the absence of the Chief Justice, by the senior Associate Justice of said Supreme Judicial Court present at the State Capitol on the first day of the term for which said Senators and Representatives shall have been elected.

Section 2. Offices incompatible with each other; election to Congress disqualifies

No person holding the office of Justice of the Supreme Judicial Court, or of any inferior court, Attorney General, district attorney, Treasurer of the State, Adjutant General, judge of probate, register of probate, register of deeds, sheriffs or their deputies, clerks of the judicial courts, shall be a member of the Legislature; and any person holding either of the foregoing offices, elected to, and accepting a seat in the Congress of the United States, shall thereby vacate said office; and no person shall be capable of holding or exercising at the same time within this State, more than one of the offices before mentioned.

Section 3. Commissions

All commissions shall be in the name of the State, signed by the Governor, attested by the Secretary or a deputy of the Secretary and have the seal of the State thereto affixed.

Section 4. Elections on the first Wednesday after first Tuesday of January may be adjourned from day to day

In case the elections, required by this Constitution on the first Wednesday after the first Tuesday of January biennially, by the 2 Houses of the Legislature, shall not be completed on that day, the same may be adjourned from day to day, until completed, in the following order: The vacancies in the Senate shall first be filled; and the Governor shall then be elected, if there be no choice by the people.

Section 5. Removal by impeachment or address

Every person holding any civil office under this State, may be removed by impeachment, for misdemeanor in office; and every person holding any office, may be removed by the Governor on the address of both branches of the Legislature. But before such address shall pass either House, the causes of removal shall be stated and entered on the journal of the House in which it originated, and a copy thereof served on the person in office, that the person may be admitted to a hearing in that person's own defense.

Section 6. Tenure of office

The tenure of all offices, which are not or shall not be otherwise provided for, shall be during the pleasure of the Governor.

Section 7. Valuation

While the public expenses shall be assessed on estates, a general valuation shall be taken at least once in 10 years.

Section 8. Taxation

All taxes upon real and personal estate, assessed by authority of this State, shall be apportioned and assessed equally according to the just value thereof.

1. Intangible property

The Legislature shall have power to levy a tax upon intangible personal property at such rate as it deems wise and equitable without regard to the rate applied to other classes of property.

2. Assessment of certain lands based on current use; penalty on change to higher use

The Legislature shall have power to provide for the assessment of the following types of real estate whenever situated in accordance with a valuation based upon the current use thereof and in accordance with such conditions as the Legislature may enact:

A. Farms and agricultural lands, timberlands and woodlands;

B. Open space lands which are used for recreation or the enjoyment of scenic natural beauty;

C. Lands used for game management or wildlife sanctuaries; and

D. Waterfront land that is used for or that supports commercial fishing activities.

In implementing paragraphs A, B, C and D, the Legislature shall provide that any change of use higher than those set forth in paragraphs A, B, C and D, except when the change is occasioned by a transfer resulting from the exercise or threatened exercise of the power of eminent domain, shall result in the imposition of a minimum penalty equal to the tax which would have been imposed over the 5 years preceding that change of use had that real estate been assessed at its highest and best use, less all taxes paid on that real estate over the preceding 5 years, and interest, upon such reasonable and equitable basis as the Legislature shall determine. Any statutory or constitutional penalty imposed as a result of a change of use, whether imposed before or after the approval of this subsection, shall be determined without regard to the presence of minerals, provided that, when payment of the penalty is made or demanded, whichever occurs first, there is in effect a state excise tax which applies or would apply to the mining of those minerals.

3. School districts

The Legislature shall have power to provide that taxes, which it may authorize a School Administrative District or a community school district to levy, may be assessed on real, personal and intangible property in accordance with any cost-sharing formula which it may authorize.

4. Watercraft

Beginning with the property tax year 1984, all watercraft as defined by the Legislature shall be exempt from taxation as personal property, provided that certain watercraft as defined by the Legislature shall be subject to an excise tax to be collected and retained by the municipalities.

5. Historic and scenic preservation

The Legislature shall have the power to provide that municipalities may reduce taxes on real property if the property owner agrees to maintain the property in accordance with criteria adopted by the governing legislative body of the municipality to maintain the historic integrity of important structures or to provide scenic view easements of significant vistas.

Section 9. Power of taxation

The Legislature shall never, in any manner, suspend or surrender the power of taxation.

Section 10. Tenure of sheriffs

Sheriffs shall be elected by the people of their respective counties, by a plurality of the votes given in on the Tuesday following the first Monday of November, and shall hold their offices for 4 years from the first day of January next after their election, unless sooner removed as hereinafter provided.

Removal of sheriffs from office and replacement

Whenever the Governor upon complaint, due notice and hearing shall find that a sheriff is not faithfully or efficiently performing any duty imposed upon the sheriff by law, the Governor may remove such sheriff from office and appoint another sheriff to serve for the remainder of the term for which such removed sheriff was elected. All vacancies in the office of sheriff, other than those caused by removal in the manner aforesaid shall be filled in the same manner as is provided in the case of judges and registers of probate.

Section 11. Attorney General

The Attorney General shall be chosen biennially by joint ballot of the Senators and Representatives in convention. Vacancy in said office occurring when the Legislature is not in session, may be filled by appointment by the Governor, subject to confirmation as required by this Constitution for Justices of the Supreme Judicial Court.

Section 12. Voting districts

The Legislature may by law authorize the dividing of towns into voting districts for all state and national elections, and prescribe the manner in which the votes shall be received, counted, and the result of the election declared.

Section 13. Bribery at elections

The Legislature may enact laws excluding from the right of suffrage, for a term not exceeding 10 years, all persons convicted of bribery at any election, or of voting at any election, under the influence of a bribe.

Section 14. Authority and procedure for issuance of bonds

The credit of the State shall not be directly or indirectly loaned in any case, except as provided in sections 14-A, 14-B, 14-C and 14-D. The Legislature shall not create any debt or debts, liability or liabilities, on behalf of the State, which shall singly, or in the aggregate, with previous debts and liabilities hereafter incurred at any one time, exceed $2,000,000, except to suppress insurrection, to repel invasion, or for purposes of war, and except for temporary loans to be paid out of money raised by taxation during the fiscal year in which they are made, and except for loans to be repaid within 12 months with federal transportation funds in amounts not to exceed 50% of transportation funds appropriated by the federal government in the prior federal fiscal year; and excepting also that whenever 2/3 of both Houses shall deem it necessary, by proper enactment ratified by a majority of the electors voting thereon at a general or special election, the Legislature may authorize the issuance of bonds on behalf of the State at such times and in such amounts and for such purposes as approved by such action; but this shall not be construed to refer to any money that has been, or may be deposited with this State by the Government of the United States, or to any fund which the State shall hold in trust for any Indian tribe. Whenever ratification by the electors is essential to the validity of bonds to be issued on behalf of the State, the question submitted to the electors shall be accompanied by a statement setting forth the total amount of bonds of the State outstanding and unpaid, the total amount of bonds of the State authorized and unissued, and the total amount of bonds of the State contemplated to be issued if the enactment submitted to the electors be ratified. For any bond authorization requiring ratification of the electors pursuant to this section, if any bonds have not been issued within 5 years of the date of ratification, then those bonds may not be issued after that date. Within 2 years after expiration of that 5-year period, the Legislature may extend, by a majority vote, the 5-year period for an additional 5 years or may deauthorize the bonds. If the

Legislature fails to take action within those 2 years, the bond issue shall be considered to be deauthorized and no further bonds may be issued. For any bond authorization in existence on November 6, 1984, and for which the 5-year period following ratification has expired, no further bonds may be issued unless the Legislature, by November 6, 1986, reauthorizes those bonds by a majority vote, for an additional 5-year period, failing which all bonds unissued under those authorizations shall be considered to be deauthorized. Temporary loans to be paid out of moneys raised by taxation during any fiscal year shall not exceed in the aggregate during the fiscal year in question an amount greater than 10% of all the moneys appropriated, authorized and allocated by the Legislature from undedicated revenues to the General Fund and dedicated revenues to the Highway Fund for that fiscal year, exclusive of proceeds or expenditures from the sale of bonds, or greater than 1% of the total valuation of the State of Maine, whichever is the lesser.

Section 14-A. Authority to insure industrial, manufacturing, fishing, and agricultural mortgage loans

For the purposes of fostering, encouraging and assisting the physical location, settlement and resettlement of industrial, manufacturing, fishing, agricultural and recreational enterprises within the State, the Legislature by proper enactment may insure the payment of mortgage loans on real estate and personal property within the State of such industrial, manufacturing, fishing, agricultural and recreational enterprises not exceeding in the aggregate $90,000,000 in amount at any one time and may also appropriate moneys and authorize the issuance of bonds on behalf of the State at such times and in such amounts as it may determine to make payments insured as aforesaid. For the purposes of this section, a documented fishing vessel or a vessel registered under state law shall be construed as real estate.

Section 14-B. Authority to insure revenue bonds of the Maine School Building Authority

In order to encourage and assist in the provision and construction of public school buildings in the State, the Legislature by proper enactment may insure the payment of revenue bonds of the Maine School Building Authority on school projects within the State not exceeding in the aggregate $6,000,000 in amount at any one time and may also appropriate moneys and authorize the issuance of bonds on behalf of the State at such times and in such amounts as it may determine to make payments insured as aforesaid.

Section 14-C. Authority to insure mortgage loans for Indian housing

For the purpose of fostering and encouraging the acquisition, construction, repair and remodeling of houses owned or to be owned by members of the 2 tribes on the several Indian reservations, the Legislature by proper enactment may insure the payment of mortgage loans on such houses not exceeding in the aggregate $1,000,000 in amount at any one time and may also appropriate moneys and authorize the issuance of bonds on behalf of the State at such times and in such amounts as it may determine to make payments insured as aforesaid.

Section 14-D. Authority to insure Maine veterans' mortgage loans, and to appropriate moneys and issue bonds for the payment of same

For the purposes of recognizing the services and sacrifices of Maine's men and women who have served their state and country through honorable service in the Armed Forces of the United States in time of war or national emergency; enlarging the opportunities for employment of Maine's veterans; insuring the preservation and betterment of the economy of the State of Maine; and stimulating the flow of private investment funds to

Maine's veterans, the Legislature by proper enactment may insure the payment of any mortgage loan to resident Maine veterans of the Armed Forces of the United States, including a business organization owned in whole or in part by a resident Maine veteran, when such loans are made in connection with such legitimate purposes and under such terms and conditions as the Legislature may determine, not exceeding in the aggregate $4,000,000 in amount at any one time and may also appropriate moneys and authorize the issuance of bonds on behalf of the State at such times and in such amounts as it may determine to make payments insured as aforesaid.

Section 15. Municipal borrowing regulated by Legislature through general law

The Legislature shall enact general law regulating the total borrowing capacity of municipal corporations.

Section 16. Seat of government

Augusta is hereby declared to be the seat of government of this State.

Section 17. Continuity of Government in case of enemy attack

Notwithstanding any general or special provision of this Constitution, the Legislature, in order to insure continuity of state and local governmental operations in periods of emergency resulting from disasters caused by enemy attack, shall have the power and the immediate duty to provide for prompt and temporary succession to the powers and duties of public offices, of whatever nature and whether filled by election or appointment, the incumbents of which may become unavailable for carrying on the powers and duties of such offices, and to adopt such other measures as may be necessary and proper for insuring the continuity of governmental operations including but not limited to the financing thereof. In the exercise of the powers hereby conferred the Legislature shall in all respects conform to the requirements of this Constitution except to the extent that in the judgment of the Legislature so to do would be impracticable or would admit of undue delay.

Section 18. Limitation on use of funds of Maine State Retirement System

All of the assets, and proceeds or income therefrom, of the Maine State Retirement System or any successor system and all contributions and payments made to the system to provide for retirement and related benefits shall be held, invested or disbursed as in trust for the exclusive purpose of providing for such benefits and shall not be encumbered for, or diverted to, other purposes. Funds appropriated by the Legislature for the Maine State Retirement System are assets of the system and may not be diverted or deappropriated by any subsequent action.

Section 18-A. Funding of retirement benefits under the Maine State Retirement System

Beginning with the fiscal year starting July 1, 1997, the normal cost of all retirement and ancillary benefits provided to participants under the Maine State Retirement System must be funded annually on an actuarially sound basis. Unfunded liabilities may not be created except those resulting from experience losses. Unfunded liability resulting from experience losses must be retired over a period not exceeding 10 years.

Section 18-B. Payment of unfunded liabilities of the Maine State Retirement System

Each fiscal year beginning with the fiscal year starting July 1, 1997, the Legislature shall appropriate funds that will retire in 31 years or less the unfunded liabilities of the Maine State Retirement System that are attributable to state employees and teachers. The unfunded liabilities referred to in this Section are those determined by the Maine State Retirement System's actuaries and certified by the Board of Trustees of the Maine State Retirement System as of June 30, 1996.

Section 19. Limitation on expenditure of motor vehicle and motor vehicle fuel revenues

All revenues derived from fees, excises and license taxes relating to registration, operation and use of vehicles on public highways, and to fuels used for propulsion of such vehicles shall be expended solely for cost of administration, statutory refunds and adjustments, payment of debts and liabilities incurred in construction and reconstruction of highways and bridges, the cost of construction, reconstruction, maintenance and repair of public highways and bridges under the direction and supervision of a state department having jurisdiction over such highways and bridges and expense for state enforcement of traffic laws and shall not be diverted for any purpose, provided that these limitations shall not apply to revenue from an excise tax on motor vehicles imposed in lieu of personal property tax.

Section 20. Mining Excise Tax Trust Fund

The principal amount of the Mining Excise Tax Trust Fund or any successor fund may not be expended unless the expenditure is approved in a separate measure by a 2/3 vote of all the members elected to each House of the Legislature and by the Governor.

Section 21. State mandates

For the purpose of more fairly apportioning the cost of government and providing local property tax relief, the State may not require a local unit of government to expand or modify that unit's activities so as to necessitate additional expenditures from local revenues unless the State provides annually 90% of the funding for these expenditures from State funds not previously appropriated to that local unit of government. Legislation implementing this section or requiring a specific expenditure as an exception to this requirement may be enacted upon the vote of 2/3 of all members elected to each House. This section must be liberally construed.

Section 22. Revenues generated by fisheries and wildlife management

The amount of funds appropriated in any fiscal year to the Department of Inland Fisheries and Wildlife, or any successor agency responsible for fisheries and wildlife management, other than commercial marine fisheries management, may not be less than the total revenues collected, received or recovered by the Department of Inland Fisheries and Wildlife, or successor agency, from license and permit fees, fines, the sale, lease or rental of property, penalties and all other revenue sources pursuant to the laws of the State administered by the department or successor agency, except that revenues received from the Federal Government may be allocated as provided by federal or state law and the Legislature may establish special funds and deposit revenues collected, received or recovered by the department or successor agency into those special funds, provided that the revenues are allocated and expended only for the purposes of those special funds as provided by law.

Section 23. State park land

State park land, public lots or other real estate held by the State for conservation or recreation purposes and designated by legislation implementing this section may not be reduced or its uses substantially altered except on the vote of 2/3 of all the members elected to each House. The proceeds from the sale of such land must be used to purchase additional real estate in the same county for the same purposes.

Section 24. Reapportionment

Congressional districts must be reapportioned as follows.

1. Procedure

Beginning in 2021 and every 10 years thereafter, when the Secretary of State has received notification of the number of congressional seats to which the State is entitled and the Federal Decennial Census population count is final, the Legislative Apportionment Commission, established every 10 years pursuant to Article IV, Part Third, Section 1-A, shall review the existing congressional districts. If the districts do not conform to Supreme Judicial Court guidelines, the commission shall reapportion the State into congressional districts.

In making such a reapportionment, the commission shall ensure that each congressional district is formed of compact and contiguous territory and crosses political subdivisions the least number of times necessary to establish districts as equally populated as possible. The commission shall submit its plan to the Clerk of the House of Representatives no later than June 1st of the year in which apportionment is required. The Legislature shall enact the submitted plan of the commission or a plan of its own in regular or special session by a vote of 2/3 of the members of each House by June 11th of the year in which apportionment is required to the Clerk of the House of Representatives. This action is subject to the Governor's approval, as provided in Article IV, Part Third, Section 2.

2. Court apportionment

If the Legislature fails to make an apportionment by June 11th, the Supreme Judicial Court shall make the apportionment within 60 days following the period in which the Legislature is required to act but fails to do so. In making the apportionment, the Supreme Judicial Court shall take into consideration plans and briefs filed by the public with the court during the first 30 days of the period in which the court is required to apportion.

3. Judicial review

The Supreme Judicial Court has original jurisdiction to hear any challenge to an apportionment law enacted by the Legislature, as registered by any citizen or group of citizens. If a challenge is sustained, the Supreme Judicial Court shall make the apportionment.

Section 25. Apportionment of county commissioner districts

County commissioner districts must be apportioned as follows.

1. Redistricting, generally

Beginning in 2021 and every 10 years thereafter, the apportionment commission established under Article IV, Part Third, Section 1-A shall review the existing county commissioner districts and, as necessary, reapportion those districts in each county to establish as nearly as practicable equally populated districts. The Speaker of the House of Representatives is responsible for calling the commission together to review the county commissioner districts. No action may be taken by the commission without a quorum of 7.

A. The apportionment commission shall divide the number of commissioners in each county into the number of inhabitants of the county, excluding foreigners not naturalized, according to the latest Federal Decennial Census or a state census previously ordered by the Legislature to coincide with the Federal Decennial Census, to determine a mean population figure for each county commissioner district. Each county commissioner district must be formed of contiguous and compact territory and must cross political subdivision lines the least number of times necessary to establish as nearly as practicable equally populated districts. Whenever the population of a municipality entitles it to more than one district, all whole districts must be drawn within the municipal boundaries. Any population remainder within the municipality must be included in a district drawn to cross the municipal boundary as long as the population remainder within the municipality is contiguous to another municipality or municipalities included in the district. Any county that already meets the standards and guidelines for equally populated districts, as established by this section, this Constitution and the Constitution of the United States, need not be reapportioned.

B. Interested parties from each county may submit redistricting plans for the commission to consider. Those plans must be submitted to the commission no later than 30 calendar days after the commission is called together by the Speaker of the House of Representatives under this subsection. The commission may hold public hearings on plans affecting each county.

C. The commission shall submit its plan to the Clerk of the House of Representatives no later than June 1st of the year in which apportionment is required. The Clerk of the House of Representatives shall submit to the Legislature, no later than January 15, 2022, and every 10th year thereafter, one legislative document to reapportion the county commissioner districts based on the plan submitted by the apportionment commission. The Legislature must enact the submitted plan or a plan of its own in regular or special session by a vote of 2/3 of the members of each House within 30 calendar days after the plan is submitted to it by the Clerk of the House of Representatives. This action is subject to the Governor's approval, as provided in Article IV, Part Third, Section 2.

2. Supreme Judicial Court.

If the Legislature fails to make an apportionment within the 30 calendar days, the Supreme Judicial Court shall make the apportionment within 60 calendar days following the period in which the Legislature is required to act but fails to do so. In making the apportionment, the Supreme Judicial Court shall consider plans and briefs filed by the public with the court during the first 30 days of the period in which the court is required to apportion.

ARTICLE X: ADDITIONAL PROVISIONS

Section 1. (See Section 7)

Section 2. (See Section 7)

Section 3. Laws now in force continue until repealed

All laws now in force in this State, and not repugnant to this Constitution, shall remain, and be in force, until altered or repealed by the Legislature, or shall expire by their own limitation.

Section 4. Amendments to Constitution

The Legislature, whenever 2/3 of both Houses shall deem it necessary, may propose amendments to this Constitution; and when any amendments shall be so agreed upon, a resolution shall be passed and sent to the selectmen of the several towns, and the assessors of the several plantations, empowering and directing them to notify the inhabitants of their respective towns and plantations, in the manner prescribed by law, at the next biennial meetings in the month of November, or to meet in the manner prescribed by law for calling and holding biennial meetings of said inhabitants for the election of Senators and Representatives, on the Tuesday following the first Monday of November following the passage of said resolve, to give in their votes on the question, whether such amendment shall be made; and if it shall appear that a majority of the inhabitants voting on the question are in favor of such amendment, it shall become a part of this Constitution.

Section 5. (See Section 7)

Section 6. Constitution to be arranged by Chief Justice of the Supreme Judicial Court; Constitution to be enrolled and printed with laws; supreme law of the State

The Chief Justice of the Supreme Judicial Court shall arrange the Constitution, as amended, under appropriate titles and in proper articles, parts and sections, omitting all sections, clauses and words not in force and making no other changes in the provisions or language thereof, and shall submit the same to the Legislature; and such arrangement of the Constitution shall be made and submitted to the regular session of the Legislature in 1973 and every 10 years thereafter unless sooner authorized by the Legislature; and the draft and arrangement, when approved by the Legislature, shall be enrolled on parchment and deposited in the office of the Secretary of State; and printed copies thereof shall be prefixed to the books containing the Revised Statutes of the State. And the Constitution, with the amendments made thereto, in accordance with the provisions thereof, shall be the supreme law of the State.

Section 7. Original sections 1, 2, 5, of Article X not to be printed; Section 5 in full force

Sections 1, 2 and 5, of Article X of the Constitution, shall hereafter be omitted in any printed copies thereof prefixed to the laws of the State; but this shall not impair the validity of acts under those sections; and said Section 5 shall remain in full force, as part of the Constitution, according to the stipulations of said section, with the same effect as if contained in said printed copies.

www.ingramcontent.com/pod-product-compliance
Lightning Source LLC
Chambersburg PA
CBHW070204230526
45471CB00002B/809